HARRIER GR5 & GR7

AERO GUIDE **26**

**British Aerospace
Harrier GR Mk 5/Mk 7**

GW01086193

INTRODUCTION

The year 1990 marks the thirtieth anniversary of a very significant event in the history of aviation: on 21 October 1960, a quiet autumnal day at Hawker's airfield at Dunsfold in the peaceful Surrey countryside, the experimental P.1127 ran up its engine in earnest and rose shakily into the air, tethered for safety. Incredible as it may seem, the direct descendants of that radical machine, the Harrier family, are still the only aircraft of their type in military service anywhere in the world, the intervening years left littered with VTOL might-have-beens, the brainchildren of well-intentioned engineers whose ideas proved, ultimately, to be unsuited to the needs of an effective air arm.

Just as, to what one might term the *incognoscenti*, any warship is automatically a battleship, so any VTOL aircraft is none other than a Harrier; a glance through the scrap books will show that this is not really the case, but as far as the public notion is concerned the contention is not so wide of the mark. The synonmity is unfortunate in a sense: whilst its general features and basic layout are more or less unchanged, the Harrier II now in service with three air arms is a *very* different machine from the GR.1 which began to equip RAF squadrons in 1969 and the GR.3 which supplanted the earlier mark in the mid-1970s. Changing the name would perhaps have driven home the fact that the Harrier II is a totally new aircraft (although it is possible to propose good reasons for not doing so!)

Unlike the first four major versions of the production Harrier, which although benefiting at the P.1127 prototype stage from US financial assistance were genuinely British aircraft, the Harrier GR.5 is the product of an Anglo-US collaborative programme, the American requirement of which has, somewhat in advance of its British counterpart, brought forth the AV-8B. Already, however, not much more than two years after it was first received into service by the Royal Air Force, the GR.5 is out of production, superseded by the even more capable GR.7. A modified nose is all that is apparent externally to distinguish the two variants, but in fact the gulf is vast again: the Mk 7 can do all that is expected of the Mk 5 but it can also do it in pitch darkness – a significant improvement in capability indeed, as will be reviewed later.

For a variety of reasons the Harrier family has never enjoyed the outstanding export kudos that it has deserved – in fact, the RAF is the only wholly land-based service to operate any of its members. More success has attended efforts to sell the aircraft to navies, its V/STOL characteristics giving sea-based platforms a powerful aerial punch without the need for an 800ft-long flight deck. Omens for the Harrier II are more promising still: apart from the massive US Marine Corps buy – the launching pad, so to speak, for the whole AV-8B/GR.5 programme – the Spanish Navy has made a purchase,

Below left: Both the original export customers for the Harrier GR.1/AV-8A are now operating the Harrier II. The US Marine Corps has over 300 of the new aircraft on order, designated AV-8B (upper photo), whilst the Spanish Navy is equipped with twelve, designated EAV-8B (lower photo). *McDonnell Douglas; Peter Scott, courtesy Rolls-Royce Magazine*
Right: The new nose profile of the Harrier GR Mk 7 is clearly revealed in this close-up view. *Geoff Lee/BAe*
Below: A GR.5 from No 3 Squadron executes a vertical landing (VL) during autumn 1989 exercises. *Phil Boyden/BAe*

the Italian Navy, after much prevarication, seems about to do so (the Sea Harrier option appears to have died) and other nations' navies are seriously interested. What is particularly energising the programme in this direction is the prospect of the Harrier II Plus, a variant with a radar set in its nose, enabling it to go hunting for both airborne and floating targets.

Has the Harrier come of age? Doubtless more work still will be wrung out of the AV-8B/GR.5 airframe (despite the British version's designation, a reconnaissance variant has yet to appear, for example), but, three decades and a generation of engineers after that first tentative hover at Dunsfold, one suspects that the ultimate expression of the Harrier concept is a long way off yet. When this aircraft arrives, it may even be enjoying a totally different name!

DESIGN & DEVELOPMENT

It is not proposed here to recount the fascinating, turbulent and finally triumphant story of the events that led to the entry of the V/STOL combat jet into squadron service, the major instalments of which have been briefly described in other volumes in the AEROGUIDE series;* rather, we may allude to the circumstances in which the GR.5 came to be adopted by the RAF and the development of the aircraft from that point.

The Harrier GR.1-to-GR.3 switch involved modest improvements: by exchanging the Pegasus 6 engine of 19,000lb thrust – via the Pegasus 10 (Mk 102) of 20,500lb in the GR.1A – for the 11 (Mk 103) of 21,500lb, better VTO performance and other benefits were achieved. In itself, this update made no discernible difference to the Harrier's looks, although coincidentally the installation of a laser rangefinder in the nose and radar warning receiver (RWR) equipment at the tail made the two marks readily distinguishable one from the other. The GR.3-to-GR.5 changeover has involved a quite fundamental redesign; even so, one study that almost came to fruition involved a more modest reappraisal of the Harrier concept.

Despite the best endeavours of the V/STOL design team at Kingston, and for all the exciting proposals for building upon the success of the vectored-thrust aircraft by producing futuristic new vertical-take-off machines, the hard realities of life were always appreciated – that the British Government would never release funds to bring such indigenous projects to maturity. With this in mind, Hawker Siddeley (now part of British Aerospace) had since 1969 been keeping in close touch with

*See AEROGUIDES 3 *Sea Harrier*, 12 *Harrier* and 16 *Harrier II*.

McDonnell Douglas at St Louis, who were themselves looking at possible successors to the GR.1s exported from Kingston to the US Marines Corps (and redesignated AV-8A). The major effort in this direction came to be the AV-16, but this programme foundered, first (it was said) because of the cost of re-engineering the airframe to accept the larger-diameter, 24,500lb thrust Pegasus engine, second because of the huge expenditure needed to produce the engine itself, and third because the requirements of the proposed user services – RAF, RN, USN, USMC – could not, in the end, be reconciled. McDonnell Douglas pursued their own studies from that point, resulting in the production AV-8B, and Hawker Siddeley looked again at the RAF's GR.3s and began to investigate what further possibilities the basic airframe held.

The upshot of Kingston's deliberations was a less innovative proposal than that championed by McDonnell Douglas, although the basic objectives were similar in outline: keep the existing Pegasus powerplant but design a new wing to increase the aircraft's range and payload. New-build aircraft could be brought into production quickly and relatively cheaply; indeed, it would be perfectly practicable to convert existing GR.3 airframes,

Below: The first Harrier GR.5 to be completed and flown was ZD318, alias DB1 (that is, the first of the two Development Batch machines), shown here at Dunsfold some time after its 30 April 1985 maiden flight. This aircraft is now (early 1990) being used for GR.7 systems integration trials by British Aerospace. *Mike Connelly/BAe*
Right: DB2 – ZD319 – first flew on 31 July 1985; it is seen here with nozzles swivelled downwards and suction relief doors fully open, slowing for the camera. *BAe*

thereby allowing funds to be reined in even further. The 'Big-Wing Harrier' – sometimes also referred to as the Harrier GR Mk 5(K) – would feature a much larger and thicker aerofoil than the GR.3's, with some 50 sq ft more area, increased fuel capacity and the ability to support four weapons pylons a side and a missile rail at each tip; the wing, which would also sport leading-edge root extensions (LERX), was still an all-metal structure. Other less obvious modifications, for example to the intakes and lift-improvement strakes, could boost payload further, whilst the Pegasus 11, with minor tinkering, could perhaps be persuaded to part with a couple of hundred more pounds' worth of thrust.

It was not to be. The 'Big-Wing Harrier' was summarily cancelled in August 1981 and the AV-8B ordered in its place; the GR.5 would now be, in part, a US-designed aircraft and not a wholly British one. The reasons for the abandonment were probably twofold: the US Marine Corps were in line for a massive AV-8B inventory (provided, President Carter had indicated, than an 'export customer' be found for the aircraft) and a substantial production run meant an attractive unit price for an RAF version; and involving Kingston in a co-manufacturing deal with McDonnell Douglas held out better employment prospects for the BAe workforce and for British industry generally, which would otherwise be concerned essentially with conversion work for a mere several dozen airframes.

Whether or not the GR.5(K) would have been a better buy for the RAF is a very good question. The AV-8B, a brand new machine, certainly has more service life ahead of it than any GR.3 conversion might have had, and it has been reported that the weight of the new metal wing could have compromised the GR.5(K)'s payload and vertical flight characteristics. However, in air-to-air combat – a high degree of agility in which was specifically called for by the RAF for its new Harrier – there is no doubt about which aircraft would be superior: with an instantaneous turn rate of 20deg/sec thanks to its

WORK SHARE

Reversing the arrangement in place for the US Marine Corps' AV-8Bs, British Aerospace is the prime contractor for Harrier GR.5 manufacture and McDonnell Douglas the subcontractor, the actual work load being split more or less evenly. The front fuselage and wing are built in the USA and shipped to Britain; manufacture of British components and assemblies is centred at Kingston, with input from other BAe factories (for example Brough, Warton and Hamble); final assembly takes place at Dunsfold. Engine production is the responsibility of Rolls-Royce.

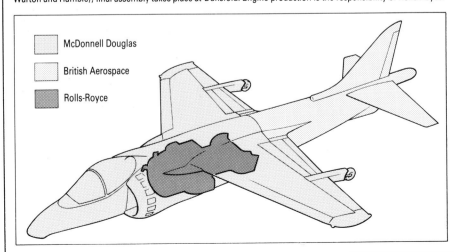

McDonnell Douglas

British Aerospace

Rolls-Royce

Far left: The Harrier GR.1 (upper photo) contrasted with the proposed 'Big-Wing Harrier' (lower photo) which around 1979–80 looked set for future RAF service. This GR.5(K) concept model shows wing-tip Sidewinder missiles and leading-edge root extensions to give the aircraft an agile dog-fighting capability, whilst the outrigger undercarriage has been moved inboard compared to the GR.1 in order to keep the wheel track to reasonable dimensions. The new wing was not the only modification proposed, updated avionics also figuring strongly in a retrofitted Harrier fleet. *John Tweddel/BAe; BAe*

Right: The wing planform of the GR.5 as finalised is seen to advantage in this air-to-air study. *Phil Boyden/BAe*

advanced aerofoil – 50 per cent up on the AV-8B's original rate – the 'Big-Wing Harrier' would have far outclassed its US counterpart in this department. Nevertheless, a number of UK-derived modifications have been incorporated into the standard AV-8B (notably the LERX – improving the turn rate), and the RAF is well pleased with its new steed.

The detail changes from the USMC version of the Harrier II called for by the British Ministry of Defence can fairly be categorised as cosmetic. Externally, the GR.5 has a deepened tip to its nose, the bulge in fact being redundant since the Miniature Infra-Red Linescan System (MIRLS) which was supposed to occupy it was never developed into a production item. More efficacious are the two extra wing pylons, aligned along the axes of the

outrigger wheel fairings, which are exclusively for occupation by AIM-9 Sidewinder missiles, giving the aircraft a self-defence capability – and, indeed, an interception capability – without penalising the air-to-ground warload. The cannon armament, when fitted, also differs: whereas the USMC aircraft sports a GAU-12/U cannon in one underbelly pod and ammunition for same in the other, the RAF has plumped for a pair of the new Royal Ordnance 25mm Aden cannon, successor to the 1953-vintage 30mm Aden which armed the GR.3. Lumps and bumps at the extremities of the airframe also distinguish the two variants, the GR.5 for example being fitted with an active-radar Missile Approach Warning (MAW) system and a different electronic countermeasures (ECM) suite from it US stablemate. The contents of the

cockpit reflect the differing requirements of the two user services, prominent amongst these being the GR.5's Ferranti moving map on the right-hand side of the main panel, requiring the relocation of various switches and instruments, and the Martin-Baker ejection seat in place of the AV-8B's Stencel SIIIS. Finally, there is one minor change concerning the engine: the US machines have had their F402 (Pegasus) powerplants de-rated from 21,750lb to 21,450lb to eke out the maintenance cycles a little.

The question of a two-seat Harrier II trainer for the RAF, long debated, has now been settled. Harrier experience in the standard T.4 trainer, plus sessions at the simulator, are currently deemed sufficient to enable converting pilots to cope with the new GR.5, and it was felt by many until recently that T.4s upgraded with night avionics to T.6 standard might have been adequate to train pilots for the specialised GR.7 mission. However, it was announced on 28 February 1990 that fourteen genuine GR.7 equivalents, designated T Mk 10 and retaining a full operational capability, are to be supplied to the RAF.

HARRIER GR.5/7 DATA

Type: Single-seat V/STOL tactical ground-attack fighter.
Powerplant: One Rolls-Royce Pegasus 11-21 (Mk 105) vectored-thrust turbofan rated at 21,750lb static thrust.
Dimensions: Overall length 46ft 4in (14.12m); wing span 30ft 4½in (9.26m); overall height 11ft 8in (3.55m); wing area (inc LERX) 239 sq ft (22.2m²).
Weights: Empty operating about 14,300lb (6485kg); maximum VTO 18,950lb (8594kg); maximum CTO 31,000lb (14,060kg).
Performance: Maximum speed 662mph (1065kph) at sea level, Mach 0.9 at altitude; typical radius (with Aden cannon, four BL755, two fuel tanks and Sidewinder) 660nm (1220km); ferry range (four tanks) 2100nm (3885km).
Armament: Two 25mm Aden cannon with 100rds each; two AIM-9L Sidewinder AAMs; up to 9200lb external ordnance (see page 32).
Service: First flight (YAV-8B) 9 November 1978, (FSD AV-8B) 5 November 1981, (GR.5) 30 April 1985, (GR.7) 29 November 1989; service entry (GR.5) 1 July 1987, (GR.7) ?1991.

Above: DBI was rolled out (and, indeed, first flown) in a raw state, the only concession to the Dunsfold artists' prowess being the temporary proclamation on the nose, in red and white. The two primer colours reflect fairly accurately the Kingston–St Louis work-split, the dark green front fuselage and wing being of US origin. *Phil Boyden/BAe*
Left: A pair of production GR.5s wait their turn for delivery to the RAF, Dunsfold, summer 1988; a Hawk two-seater destined for the Royal Saudi Air Force is visible in the background. Although Kingston is the principle centre for GR.5 manufacture, components are also fabricated at other BAe premises; major assemblies are taken by road to Dunsfold for final assembly and flight testing.
Right, top: Pre-flight inspection completed, BAe's Steve Thomas – of Falklands War fame – climbs aboard to deliver ZD349 to No 233 OCU at Wittering, where it would be coded 'H' and have its unit marking applied to the nose . . .
Right: . . . as shown in this air-to-air view of sister-ship ZD324. *Geoff Lee/BAe*

While by no means yesterday's aircraft, the GR.5 is not, in fact, the latest mark of Harrier to be built for the RAF: even as the first Development Batch GR.5, DB1, was being assembled, plans were being formulated for the production of a successor. All Harriers hit hard and hit fast, but they can only do so during the hours of daylight and in reasonable weather; but with the changeover, involving the 63rd aircraft (that is, the 61st production aircraft) and subsequent is machines, to building GR.7s instead of GR.5s, a whole new dimension has been added to the Harrier's capabilities – the significance of which cannot be understated.

The key to this new dimension to Harrier operations ies with two new pieces of equipment, a forward-looking nfra-red (FLIR) system and a pair of night vision goggles NVGs). Neither of these concepts is particularly new, but in the GR.7 they come together for the first time in a Western European jet aircraft, honed to perfection via a relentless series of trials conducted on both sides of the Atlantic and involving, in their separate programmes, British Aerospace, McDonnell Douglas, the US Marine Corps, the Royal Aircraft Establishment (RAE) at Bedford ('Night Bird' project) and the Strike Attack Operational Evaluation Unit (SAOEU) at A&AEE Boscombe Down. In 1987–88 McDonnell Douglas flight-tested the first Harrier II to be fitted with a full night attack suite, and over 200 hours of experience were chalked up as a result; the USMC's Night Attack Harrier, broadly comparable to the GR.7 in its sensor outfit, entered service in 1989.

FLIR is a form of thermal imaging equipment, well known to modern-day tank commanders and to crew members of such aircraft as the two-seat A-6E/TRAM and other night/bad weather attack types – especially including battlefield helicopters. In contrast to, for example, a standard television camera (and, for that matter, the human eye), which gathers light in order to create its transmitted image, FLIR relies on detecting temperature differences in and around the object under surveillance and converts the information thus received into a monochrome TV-type image; in other words, it is receptive to much longer wavelengths of the electromagnetic spectrum than those of visible light. The more sophisticated the IR equipment, the greater, generally speaking, its sensitivity, the smaller the variations in radiated energy that can be detected and the more detailed the image projected into the pilot's cockpit. The IR sensor depends upon the fact that all objects, even 'cold' ones, transmit electromagnetic radiation at different levels. Early equipment could pick out, for

Left: What the well-dressed Harrier pilot will look like in the years ahead, his NITE-OP night vision goggles (NVGs) giving him capabilities that only a sustained diet of carrots could, reputedly, have done in the past! Nobody claims that NVGs give the same image that a brilliant summer's day can provide, but the GR.7 driver will be able to fly sorties at any time, day or night, except in really nasty weather. *Ferranti, courtesy BAe*
Below: ZD438 shows the GR.7 external configuration though is technically a GR.5A – it is fitted for the new night avionics but has not yet had them installed. Cannon pods will be standard for the GR.7, and this aircraft also has a centreline pylon. *Geoff Lee/BAe*

example, a running engine from a vehicle, the comparative warmth of a parked aircraft in relation, perhaps, to its surroundings and so on, but today's imagery approaches in quality that of a light-derived photograph, so sensitive is the apparatus now available.

Although FLIR can be installed in swivel-headed pods or turret-like devices to enable wide field-of-view (FOV) scanning to be accomplished, in the Harrier GR.7 the system, made by GEC Sensors, is fixed, housed in a fairing on top of the nose cone, and thus can only capture images directly ahead of the aircraft. The pilot, however, has to have something more than 'tunnel vision' while flying his night-time sortie: he needs, for example, to be able to locate landmarks en route to the target, and he needs a wide FOV to help him keep a wary eye open for 'bogeys'. To aid him further, therefore, his helmet is equipped with Ferranti NITE-OP (Night Imaging Through Electro Optics Package) night-vision goggles. In simple terms, NVGs function by intensifying optical light and delivering the enhanced images thus produced direct to the pilot's eyes. Even on so-called pitch black nights, there is always some ambient light, enabling the unaided eye to identify some features of the surroundings. The NVGs, powered by small batteries and looking for all the world like a complex pair of binoculars, convert incoming light (photons) to electrons by means of photocathode lenses, enhance the electrons via a multiplier, and re-transmit the intensified beams, inverted in order to 'correct' the image, as photons (i.e. optical light) to the eyepieces; since they are part of the helmet, the goggles follow the pilot's line of sight rather than the aircraft's fore-and-aft axis and thus enable him to view the outside world, while not exactly as if in daylight, at least in sufficient detail to give him a comprehensive general picture. As well as enabling the GR.7 pilot to navigate to and locate his target, equally as importantly he can do so flying a terrain-masked profile, as in daylight.

While some NVG systems allow the pilot the option of normal viewing (the eyepieces being set some distance from his face so that he can peer beneath them), the NITE-OP does not, and thus the GR.7's cockpit instrumentation and lighting system has had to be modified from that in the GR.5; to use the jargon, the new cockpit set-up is NGC (night-goggle-compatible). In

Above: The USMC's Night Attack Harrier, now in production at St Louis, is broadly similar in concept to the GR.7 and also uses a FLIR system designed by GEC. This trials aircraft, sporting the 'XE' code of VX-5 'Vampires' on its tail, totes low-drag bombs and a pair of Maverick missiles. *McDonnell Douglas, courtesy BAe*

addition to the standard controls (see pages 30–31) and the FLIR image projected on to his HUD, the GR.7 driver has a new GEC Avionics Digital Colour Map Unit (DCMU), viewed on a Smiths Industries Multi-Purpose Display (MPD), which replaces the moving map display featured in all RAF Harriers to date and also functions as a standby or alternative MPD to that fitted to the left-hand side of the main panel. He also has different life-support equipment compared to that provided in the GR.5 – nuclear/biological/chemical (NBC) warfare protection, and on-board oxygen generation with an oxygen/air mixture control.

The advantages of the new equipment in the GR.7 are self-evident: for the first time the tactical squadron commander can order close-support missions at any time, day or night, except in the very foulest weather – an option that has so far only been available to commanders of interdictor (deep strike) aircraft like the Tornado GR.1. Thus movements of troops, supplies etc are now subject to attack at any time, not merely during the hours of daylight (which in a Northern European winter can be as few as five or six in every twenty-four).

Below: Virtually indistinguishable from the GR.5 apart from its nose 'blisters', the Mk 7 is expected to enter service in 1991 in RAF Germany. *Geoff Lee/BAe*

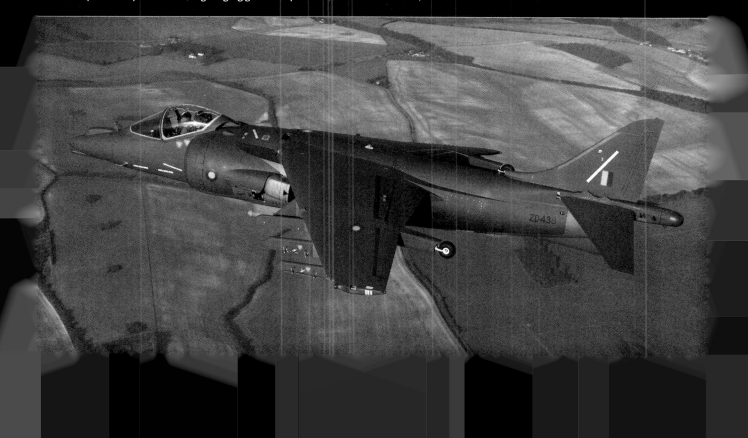

TWO PLUS

Despite the recent innovations that have turned the Harrier II into a very capable night attacker, it is still essentially a single-role aircraft: the GR.5/7's heat-seeking Sidewinders notwithstanding, its task is the close support of friendly troops, delivering air-to-ground ordnance against fixed targets previously identified by aerial or ground reconnaissance, located visually by the pilot and designated either by the ARBS in the aircraft's nose or by a ground controller. Perhaps somewhat ungenerously, the US Marines refer to the Harrier II as a 'bomb truck', and, true enough, it cannot search for, locate and hit moving targets either in the air or on the ground. Its ordnance, therefore, is either of the purely ballistic variety or, if guided, of a type that relies on 'eyeball' acquisition in the first place.

Equipped with a modern multi-mode radar set, the Harrier II would be transformed into a potent multi-mission combat aircraft. Such a programme has long been mooted – after all, the Blue Fox-equipped Sea Harrier, the stuff of.legend following its exploits in the South Atlantic back in 1982, has demonstrated what can be achieved by modifying the first-generation Harrier along these lines – and at the 1987 Paris Air Show the new variant was officially announced. Christened Harrier II Plus, the aircraft is at the moment a private venture, its development thus far funded entirely by British Aerospace and McDonnell Douglas.

Although the particular piece of radar equipment to be installed has yet to be finally decided, the Hughes AN/APG-65 would appear to be the leading contender. Compact, powerful, up-to-date and proven in service, it could, with minimal modification, be slotted into the Harrier II and has the advantage of being totally familiar both to the US Marine Corps and to McDonnell Douglas at St Louis, where hundreds of sets have been fitted into the noses of F-18 Hornets. Applied to the Harrier II, the APG-65 would offer the pilot a very wide range of modes in both the air-to-air and air-to-ground role, giving coverage at all altitudes and including a 'look up' and 'look down' capability, discriminating, in the case of the latter, fast-moving targets from ground 'clutter' thanks to its pulse-doppler facility. Other radar equipment could doubtless be installed in the II Plus, GEC/Ferranti's Blue Vixen – selected for BAe's own Sea Harrier Mk 2 programme for the Royal Navy – being an obvious candidate.

Just as a radar set will enable the Harrier II pilot to locate targets beyond visual range, a complementary set of BVR weapons will enable him to engage them successfully. Chief among these are the AIM-120 AMRAAM, the proposed successor to Sparrow and Sky Flash, for medium-range air-to-air encounters, and Sea Eagle and Harpoon, for 'fire-and-forget' attacks on enemy ships. Sidewinder and the underbelly cannon armament would be retained, for close-range engagements, optionally slaved to the radar equipment to give the pilot enemy range, position and velocity data.

Although the US Marine Corps have issued an operational requirement for the Harrier II Plus, no firm orders for the aircraft have to date been received. However, a development aircraft is being built, with its first flight scheduled to take place in 1992.

Above: Front-runner in the Harrier II Plus radar stakes is the well-known Hughes APG-65, currently in widespread service since it equips the F-18 Hornet. McDonnell Douglas have thus had a close relationship with the system for many years; for the II Plus, the company has already built a cockpit simulator that utilises it. *Hughes*

Right: A provisional three-view drawing of the Harrier II Plus, shown with US-style gun pods, two Sidewinders, four Advanced Medium-Range Air-to-Air Missiles (AMRAAM) and a pair of underwing fuel tanks. The FLIR system adopted for the night-attack AV-8B/GR.7 is retained (as would be night-vision goggles for the pilot). Apart from the new nose radome, the principal external change is the extended intake duct at the base of the tailfin. Wing span and overall height are unchanged from the original Harrier II, but overall length is quoted as 47ft 9in (14.55m), an increase of some 1ft 5in (0.43m).

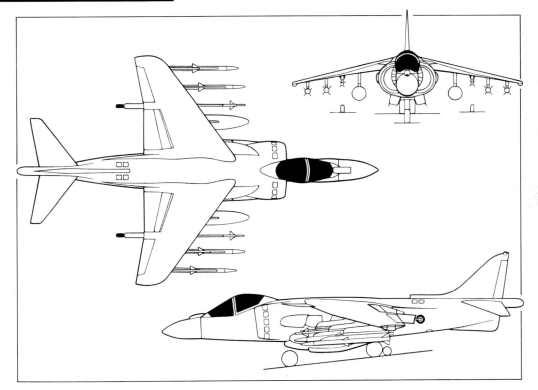

Page 12

STRUCTURE

Despite its overall general resemblance to earlier marks of the Harrier, structurally the GR.5 is a very different beast. The principal change is that, in contrast to the all-metal GR.1/3 and Sea Harrier, the Harrier II utilises carbon-fibre composite (CFC) materials over a very significant proportion of its airframe – 25 per cent by weight in fact. The multi-spar torque box for the wing, for example, is mostly CFC, with composite skinning, and only the leading-edge skinning, the wing tips and certain ribs and fittings which have a complex loading are fabricated from metals. The flaps and ailerons are about 65 per cent CFC by weight. Composites are also employed for the fuselage forward of the intakes, the overwing fairing, the engine-bay doors, the tailplane, the rudder, the outrigger fairings and the underbelly strakes. As in the GR.1/3, titanium is used along the fuselage aft of the hot nozzles and locally, inboard, on the flaps, the remainder of the airframe being for the most part aluminium alloy. In all, it is estimated that the use of CFC saves 480lb in weight with strakes fitted (330lb for the wing alone) compared with an equivalent metal structure.

As well as saving weight, the use of CFC results in better resistance to fatigue and corrosion and offers greater latitude for aerodynamic tailoring. Thus, for example, it can improve the efficiency of the aerofoil itself, generating more lift than a conventionally engineered shape; in addition, the Harrier II's aerofoil section is of the 'supercritical' type, allowing greater thickness (hence more fuel capacity) for a given performance than a wing of conventional metal construction. The empty weight of the GR.5 is about 14,300lb, only some 1500lb more than that of the GR.3, yet it can, on a short take-off and landing (STOL) mission, carry a load about 1½ tons heavier, including, if required, 44 per cent more fuel – resulting in a significantly increased radius of action compared to the earlier Harrier marks.

Close attention was paid in the design of the AV-8B/GR.5 to increasing lift, and not only by reconfiguring the wing. The new underfuselage Lift Improvement Devices

Left: The use of carbon-fibre composite (CFC) material in the Harrier II saves weight, avoids the problems of metal fatigue and corrosion and, in the case of the wing, offered greater scope for aeroelastic tailoring than any kind of metal could provide. Virtually the entire forward fuselage and all but a small proportion of the wing are CFC: here DBI's front fuselage is aligned with its UK-built rear prior to mating. The front ends arrive from St Louis with most of the cockpit instrumentation *in situ*; the British avionics etc are installed later. *Phil Boyden/BAe*
Below: Rear fuselages nearing completion at Kingston, their yellowish primer testifying to their metal construction. *Geoff Lee/BAe*

(LIDs) were developed by McDonnell Douglas to replace the somewhat embryonic strakes apparent on earlier versions of the Harrier. The arrangement of these LIDs forms, as it were, a 'pressure box' beneath the fuselage, confining a proportion of the jet efflux 'fountain' and so contributing additional VTO lift; a retractable cross-fence ('dam') forward reduces the amount of hot air from the efflux that can swirl up into the engine intake, so keeping thrust degradation to a minimum. In total, these underbelly features are worth about 1000lb of thrust and are aided by 'positive-circulation' flaps which, for VSTOL, are drooped at an angle of 61.7 degrees. Further efficiency has been brought about by the introduction of 'zero-scarf' front ('cold' air) nozzles, which improve the collimation of the efflux in vertical flight and also give benefits in STO performance, as well as reducing the adverse effect of the exhaust on inboard weapons when carried. Finally, both the main intakes and their auxiliary doors were redesigned, adding some 200lb extra equivalent thrust to the engine.

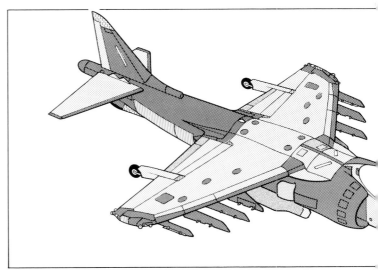

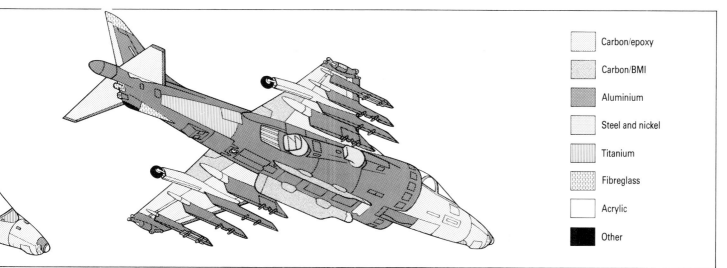

Carbon/epoxy

Carbon/BMI

Aluminium

Steel and nickel

Titanium

Fibreglass

Acrylic

Other

Top: Details of the materials used in the construction of the Harrier II. As percentages of the total structural weight, CFC accounts for about 25, metallics about 70, acrylic about 1.75, fibreglass about 0.25 and 'other' (e.g. rubber) about 3.

Above: DB1 up on its maiden sortie, unpainted save for factory identification and the necessary safety/ rescue markings, plus the cold-nozzle angle calibration. *Geoff Lee/BAe*

Left: The unique nose profile of the GR.5, showing the fairing intended to accommodate the Miniature Infra-Red Linescan System (MIRLS) but actually occupied by ballast since this equipment programme was cancelled in 1985. The nose glazing protects the US-designed Angle Rate Bombing System (ARBS).

Below: The GR.7's nose fairly bristles with sensors, the ARBS 'eye' now complemented by the FLIR seeker above and a pair of Zeus antenna domes beneath. *Jim Moore/BAe*

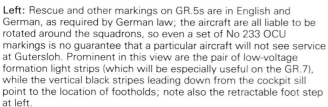

Left: Rescue and other markings on GR.5s are in English and German, as required by German law; the aircraft are all liable to be rotated around the squadrons, so even a set of No 233 OCU markings is no guarantee that a particular aircraft will not see service at Gutersloh. Prominent in this view are the pair of low-voltage formation light strips (which will be especially useful on the GR.7), while the vertical black stripes leading down from the cockpit sill point to the location of footholds; note also the retractable foot step at left.
Above left: A glimpse into the starboard intake, showing the colour demarcation between the white interior and the NATO green exterior.

Above right: Suction relief doors, port side, showing the normal attitude of these fittings on a parked aircraft. The doors deliver extra air to the compressor face during low-speed and hovering manoeuvres, enabling the engine to produce more thrust.
Below left: Starboard 'zero-scarf' forward nozzle and its aerodynamic fairing, with oil drain below and fuel vent beneath that.
Below centre: Port forward nozzle. The calibration gives a visual indication of the nozzle setting to ground crews. The GR.5's fuelling point is shown here, as is the port LERX.
Below right: View along the fuselage, port side; note the external power supply, for ground maintenance purposes.

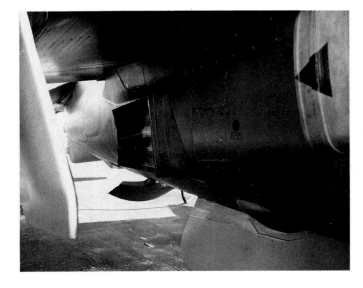

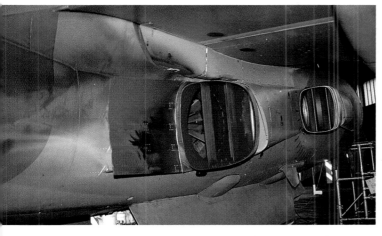

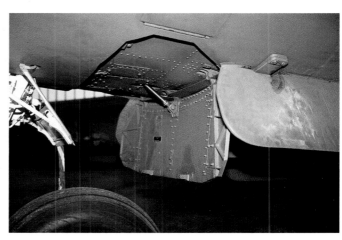

Opposite page top: Massive Lift Improvement Devices (LIDs) along the belly of the GR.5 harness some of the jet efflux during short or vertical take-offs and by increasing its ground effect add considerably to the lift generated.

Opposite page centre: The starboard LID (left photo), showing the bulky fairings over the main attachment points. Gun-armed Harriers exchange their LIDs for aerodynamic pods (right photo) which again are designed so as to enhance ground effect. Unlike their US equivalents, the GR.5's gun pods are not fitted with ventral strakes.

Opposite page bottom: Views of the 'hot' nozzle and fairing, port side; note the typical Harrier exhaust streaks.

Above left: The starboard nozzles. The ribbed plates shield the fuselage from the hottest temperatures.

Above: The retractable dam forward of the LIDs/pods helps to contain the ground effect and to keep hot gases away from the main intakes.

Left: Detail of the air brake, situated behind the main wheel bay.

Below: The anhedral wing and outrigger undercarriage arrangement recall the design of the original Harrier.

THE
JET

SQN LDR J G BAYNTON

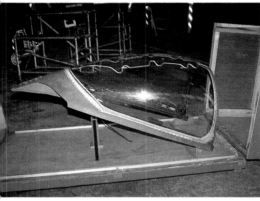

The arrival in service of a new aircraft, particularly the first one or two examples of that aircraft, obviously heralds a period of great activity within the receiving unit, and such was the case with the Harrier GR.5 (like the original Harrier, known to all in the trade' as 'The Jet'). The photographs featured in this spread were taken in April 1988 and show ZD323/'A' and ZD324/'B', the first two GR.5s to be delivered to the RAF; 'A' is being used as a non-flying ground instructional aircraft and 'B' is taking a day off normal duties to have its ejection seat investigated. The GR.5 Conversion Team (GR5CT) at RAF Wittering which had these aircraft on charge was composed of four experienced officers from the OCU, responsible for smoothing the transition from GR.3 flying to GR.5 flying; no special unit markings, official or unofficial, were carried by GR5CT aircraft.

Left top: An overwing view of a No 1 Squadron GR.5 undergoing maintenance, showing the position of the 12in-diameter roundel and the 'no step' warning on the flap.
Left bottom: A view of the rear fuselage and tail empennage. Though of the same general shape, the tail fin is larger than that of the GR.3, whilst the geometry of the horizontal stabilisers has also been revised.

Above: Head-on photo shows the spacing of the eight wing pylons and the compact undercarriage layout. *Andy Lawson/BAe*
Below: Wing details. The row of vortex generators is evident (left), as is the aerodynamic 'twist' of the aerofoil (right).
Bottom: Starboard inner pylons (left) and port outers (right), showing design variations to accommodate the requirements of drooping the flaps and ailerons.

Top left: The all-moving stabilisers are primarily of composite construction, with metal leading edges and kick ribs.

Top right: A formation strip light dominates the vertical tail. The intake at the base of the fin gulps air to help cool air-conditioning equipment.

Above: The starboard stabiliser. The deflection scale on the fuselage aids ground checks; the opening beneath is the heat-exchanger exhaust.

Above right: The ventral fin sports a tail bumper at its base and a pair of ECM/RWR antennae at the trailing edge. The standard oily streak is particularly well defined on this aircraft!

Right: The tail cone features yaw RCVs, navigation light and, aft, the radome for the Missile Approach Warning (MAW) system. Most of the aircraft's panels are numbered, with 'L' or 'R' for left or right – an inexpensive way of saving valuable (and costly) maintenance time.

Opposite page: Aspects of the Harrier II's nose undercarriage gear, which retracts forwards. Little changed from that of the earlier Harriers, it is of the levered suspension type and is equipped with nitrogen bottles (note symbol on door) for emergency extension.

Above: The twin main wheels again differ little from those of earlier members of the Harrier family.
Left: The large mainwheel doors are normally open only for a few seconds during the in-flight retraction or extension sequence though of course can be lowered for ground maintenance purposes, as here.
Below: A rarely seen Harrier feature: inside the mainwheel bay.
Right: Four photos depicting the outrigger undercarriage. These units are quite different from those of the GR.3, being longer, having retraction struts forward instead of aft and being housed in more streamlined fairings complete with miniature bay doors. Lugs both here and on the nosegear facilitate lash-down when the aircraft are deployed on board ship (as are No 1 Squadron's from time to time).

POWERPLANT

The Pegasus, now in continuous development for some 35 years, is still the only production vectored-thrust jet engine in the world and it is unique to, and inseparably associated with, the Harrier family. The very first engine was bench-run in 1959, yielding 9000lb of thrust, and the first installation was the Pegasus 3 of 14,000lb, which powered the P.1127 and successfully blessed the airframe/powerplant marriage which still thrives in the GR.5 and 7.

As related earlier, the Pegasus II (Mk 105) installed in the GR.5 (designated F402-RR-406 for AV-8Bs) differs little in general arrangement – and not at all in overall dimensions – from the Mk 104 fitted in the Sea Harrier, which is itself a navalised (anti-corrosion) variant of the Mk 103 that powers the GR.3. It was the very great cost of the 24,500lb thrust Pegasus 15 earmarked for the proposed AV-16 (together with the necessary fuselage redesign) that was a major factor in the decision to abandon the development of that aircraft and to upgrade the existing Harrier's airframe rather than its engine.

However, the Mk 105 shows important improvements over the Mk 103, particularly with regard to its reliability record and maintenance demands. As in the Mk 104, aluminium has been substituted for magnesium in the main casing, to improve resistance to corrosion (US Marine 'harrying' takes place from on board ship as well as from land bases), while other improvements include wider-root first-stage fan blades (giving reduced stress levels); stiffened first-stage stator vanes (alleviating flutter during high-speed low-level operations); trunnion-mounted second-stage stators and an improved jet-pipe temperature (JPT) thermocoupling (reducing vibration and thus prolonging engine life); and better cooling facilities (reducing engine wear). All add up to a 500-hour 'hot-end' inspection cycle and a 1000-hour time between overhauls (TBO) – easing

considerably the cost of maintaining the engine. The Mk 105 is also fitted with a Digital Engine Control System (DECS), a propulsion management unit which monitors the performance of the powerplant at all times during a sortie. Developed by Dowty/Smiths Industries Controls in partnership with Rolls-Royce, BAe and McDonnell Douglas, it automatically adjusts the engine's thrust settings, taking into account aircraft speed and altitude, within the limitations imposed by, for example, rpm, jet-pipe temperature and acceleration; previously these functions had to be monitored by the pilot via a hydro-mechanical fuel control unit, a jet-pipe temperature limited (JPTL) and a pressure ratio limiter (PRL), and the end result is more 'carefree' throttle control for the pilot.

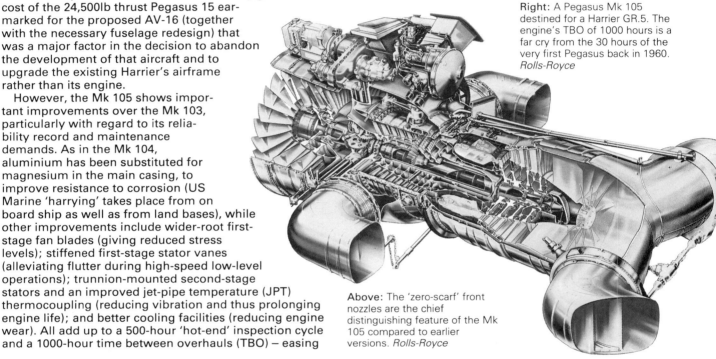

Right: A Pegasus Mk 105 destined for a Harrier GR.5. The engine's TBO of 1000 hours is a far cry from the 30 hours of the very first Pegasus back in 1960. *Rolls-Royce*

Above: The 'zero-scarf' front nozzles are the chief distinguishing feature of the Mk 105 compared to earlier versions. *Rolls-Royce*

PEGASUS 11-61

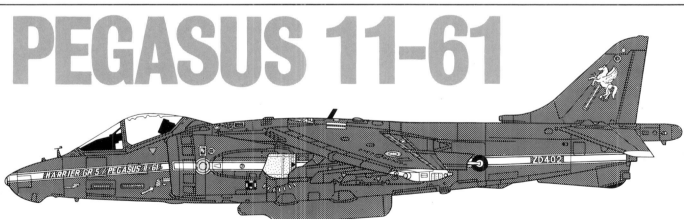

In prospect for installation in Harrier IIs is the Pegasus 11-61, derived from the 11-21 or Mk 105 (F402-RR-406) now flying in GR.5s and AV-8Bs. Featuring a new front fan of increased pressure ratio and improved high-pressure (HP) and low-pressure (LP) turbines able to accept the higher temperatures brought about by greater combustive efficiency, the new version of the engine is rated at 23,390lb – an increase of some 10 per cent over the Mk 105 figure. The 11-61 has been ordered for the USMC, with first deliveries in 1990, and is expected in the future to power the RAF's GR.7. It can, in fact, be retrofitted to any Harrier airframe since its dimensions (11ft 5in long overall and 4ft across the fan casing) are unchanged from those of the Mk 103/4/5; it is also available as a kit for upgrading 11-21s to 11-61 standard. Quite apart from the increased 'poke', the new Pegasus reduces still further the engine maintenance demands, allowing, for example, 'hot-end' inspections every 1000 hours.

After being bench-tested as the XG-15, a pre-production 11-61 was installed in GR.5 ZD402 (see accompanying illustrations), which promptly set four new time-to-height Class H (Jet Lift) world records, including a 0-to-12,000m (0–39,370ft) zoom in 126.6 seconds. The aircraft first flew on 9 June 1989, finished in a special 'midnight blue' scheme concocted to a one-off Dunsfold recipe and adorned with white fuselage, wing-tip and tailplane trim, a white pegasus on the tailfin and the well-known BAe logo on the engine inspection doors. Fuselage and wing roundels were pink and pale blue.

COCKPIT

I t is in the cockpit that the hardened GR.3 man will, in the GR.5, discover a whole new world. Quite apart from the fact that it is roomier and gives the pilot an eyeline 10in higher than that in the older aircraft (he can now see the wing tips and two outermost pylons from his seat instead of having everything blocked off by the big intakes), the instrumentation is 1980s-style instead of 1960s. The Smiths Industries 425SUM1 head-up display (HUD) and its associated up-front control (UFC) push-buttons from the AV-8B are there, as is the multi-purpose display (MPD) screen to his left, offering him a variety of display modes, including navigation, stores management, weapons delivery, engine/fuel data and radar warning. Right of centre, however, is the Ferranti moving map display familiar from GR.3 days. Receiving computer-aided data from the Litton AN/ASN-130 inertial navigation system – the proposed Ferranti FIN 1075 INS has been a little late in coming on stream – situated under his feet, this provides the pilot with a projected physical map, fed from a pre-inserted cassette, of his sortie area. The recorded map can cover a 1000-mile square of territory and is accurate to within one ground-mile for each hour of flying time. The map is being displaced in the GR.7 by GEC Avionics' DCMU, as noted on pages 10–11.

Dials are conspicuous by their relative absence, confined to flight instruments (altitude, speed, AOA, compass with course/heading/distance, etc, plus clock) situated centrally, behind the HOTAS (hands-on-throttle-and-stick) type control grip. The side consoles are more familiar, with fuel, external lighting, oxygen etc switches to the left and communications, cockpit environment and power supply switches to the right; the throttle and nozzle actuator lever, the latter marked in 5-degree increments, are of course still side by side on the left console, but just ahead of these is the pilot's delight – the control panel for the stability augmentation and attitude hold system (SAAHS), which, first, provides auto-stabilisation throughout the flight envelope and, second, acts as an autopilot during take-off, landing and transition, with automatic altitude, attitude and heading hold – especially valuable during the low-speed manoeuvres vital to the STOVL aircraft.

A high-tech ejection seat, the Martin-Baker Type 12 (more accurately described by the manufacturers as an 'escape system' rather than a seat), is installed in the Harrier GR.5 – its first application. Derived from the Type 10L which is found in such aircraft as the Swedish Gripen and the Italo-Brazilian AMX, the Type 12 is, like most modern seats, a 'zero–zero' system (i.e. it can function from an aircraft parked on the ground – zero speed and zero altitude) but has one revolutionary feature. It is fitted with a speed sensing device that permits a delayed main parachute deployment to ensure that the seat is fully stabilised and decelerated by means of a drogue before descent proper begins.

Below: The Harrier GR.5 pilot is equipped with the Martin-Baker Type 12 ejection seat, which has retractable, headbox-mounted sensors that sample the airspeed during escape and modify the operation of the drogue and personnel parachute accordingly. *Martin-Baker Aircraft Co*
Right: Traditional dials are hard to find in the GR.5's roomy cockpit, replaced by the TV-type multi-purpose display (MPD) at left. Note the Smiths Industries HUD on the coaming. *Andy Lawson/BAe*

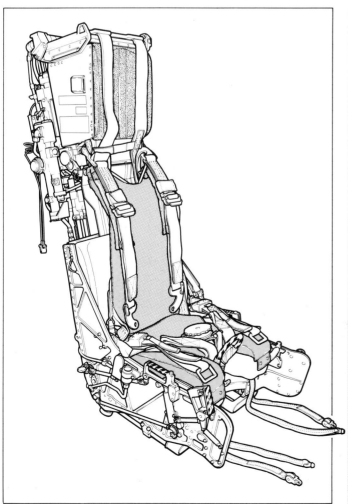

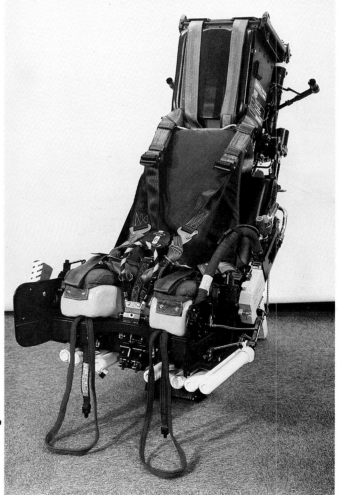

WEAPONS & STORES

Of the roughly 14,500lb available to the Harrier GR.5 for fuel and weapons, some 9200lb takes the form of external stores, divided among nine stations – four per wing plus one centreline – and the two underbelly cannon pods. Apart from the pods, which enclose a new mark of Aden gun (as illustrated overleaf), the only really new equipment currently available to the RAF's Harrier force is the AIM-9L all-aspect Sidewinder missile. True, GR.3s were wired up for Sidewinders during the 1982 Falklands campaign, but the missile has never really been a standard fit. The dedicated AAM pylons are unique to the RAF Harrier II and are located between the inner and intermediate stations on each wing, aligned with the outrigger undercarriage fairings. Theoretically, further AIM-9s can, as with the USMC's AV-8B, be carried on other stores points, but the Harrier commander is unlikely to wish to compromise the aircraft's main role, that of ground attack/close support.

The standard range of GR.3 stores is also available to the GR.5 and 7 – Hunting BL755 cluster bombs, free-fall or retarded general-purpose (GP) 500lb and 1000lb bombs, Matra 155 rocket pods (each with eighteen 68mm SNEB rockets) and the usual series of CBLS (practice bomb carriers). The inner and intermediate pylons are plumbed for fuel, though reports of GR.5s wearing drop tanks have, to date, been hard to come by; the aircraft's much improved range makes their carriage on UK training sorties less necessary than for the GR.3 and their use is confined chiefly to ferry sorties.

Weapons in prospect for the RAF's new Harrier include the European-sponsored Advanced Short-Range AAM (ASRAAM), a replacement for Sidewinder which, first planned in the mid-1970s, has had a difficult and protracted development history. The BL755 was due to be replaced by the Modular Stand-Off Weapon (MSOW) in the mid to late 1990s but this programme has now fallen under the axe and either the Marconi Brimstone (a modified US Hellfire) or the Hunting Smart Weapon Anti-Armour (SWAARM), both of which have a stand-off capability, seems likely to be adopted, although at the

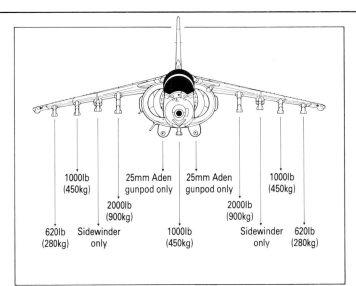

1000lb (450kg)   25mm Aden gunpod only   25mm Aden gunpod only   1000lb (450kg)

2000lb (900kg)   2000lb (900kg)

620lb (280kg)   Sidewinder only   1000lb (450kg)   Sidewinder only   620lb (280kg)

Left: Two photos showing GR.5 ZD346 on weapons proving trials, with seven Improved BL755 Cluster Bomb Units (CBU) and a pair of AIM-9G Sidewinder AAMs. *Phil Boyden/ BAe*

Above: GR.5 pylon loadings.

Above right: The standard Harrier CBLS-200 (Carrier, Bomb, Light Store) is seen here on the starboard intermediate pylon. The tiny practice bombs housed within it make for low-cost weapons training – they have the same ballistic properties as full-sized bombs.

Right: A No 3 Squadron GR.5 armed to the teeth with ordnance – 25mm cannon pods, inert CBUs, a Sidewinder acquisition round and, outboard, a Phimat chaff/flare dispenser. *Courtesy Alan Carlaw*

Below: ZD324 sporting a pair of Sidewinder acquisition rounds. *Geoff Lee/BAe*

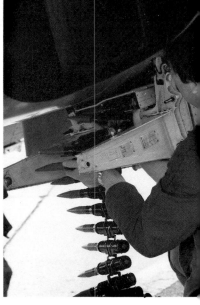

Above left and right: Testing the feed mechanism on a trial 25mm Aden installation on one of the two Development Batch Harrier GR.5s; the rounds here are a TP type, with blue projectile heads and black cases. *Courtesy Royal Ordnance*

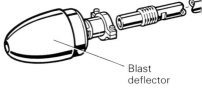

Blast
deflector

Left: The first live AIM-9 Sidewinder firing by a GR.5 on operational duty was achieved by aircraft '06' of No 1 Squadron in June 1989. The test shoot was carried out at low level against a Jindvik drone, the aircraft flying from Strike Command's Air-to-Air Missile Establishment at RAF Valley in Anglesey. *Geoff Lee/BAe*
Right: The GR.5's dedicated AAM pylon, unique to RAF Harrier IIs. Sidewinders can in fact be fitted to the intermediate and outer pylons but this particular combat load is unlikely to be seen very often.

time of writing a decision on these systems had yet to be taken.

Prominent in the nose of the GR.5 and 7 is the Hughes AN/ASB-19 Angle Rate Bombing System (ARBS), a combined tracker which in its TV mode projects target angle rate data into the cockpit to ensure accuracy of weapons delivery in a single pass. In its laser mode the ARBS can lock on to a target illuminated by a ground controller, with the obvious result. One of the most

innovative features of the aircraft, however, is Marconi's Zeus electronic countermeasures (ECM) system. Fitted internally – and thereby obviating the need to tie up valuable pylon space with an external pod – the system integrates radar warning receivers (RWR) with an automatic jammer, able to respond via its 'memory' of known emitters in order to confuse a would-be attacker. It will also automatically trigger chaff and flares to combat, respectively, radar-guided and heat-seeking missiles.

ADEN CANNON

Developed by Royal Ordnance Nottingham from the company's ill-fated 25mm Straden – itself developed from the production 30mm Aden as fitted to Harrier GR.3s – the new 25mm Aden is a gas-operated revolver-type cannon firing standard NATO projectiles. The Harrier GR.5 represents the first RAF service application of the weapon, although the gun is also earmarked for the Hawk 200. The ammunition is of the disintegrating-link variety and is percussion-fired; unlike the AV-8B installation, the rounds are accommodated in the same pod as the gun proper. High-Explosive (HE), Armour-Piercing (AP), AP Discarding Sabot (APDS) and APHE Incendiary rounds are available, plus Training Practice (TP) and Multi-Purpose (MP) types.

Left: The 25mm pod on the port side of an operational GR.5, as viewed from the rear. The pods are manufactured by BAe at Hamble.

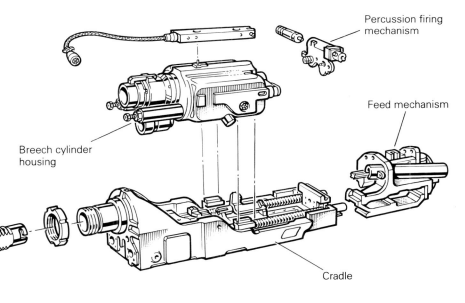

Specifications
Type: Gas-operated revolver
Calibre: 25mm
Barrel length: 66.9in (1700mm)
Barrel weight: 41.9lb (19kg)
Gun length: 90in (2285mm)

Total system weight (twin-pod installation, 200rds): 948lb (430kg)
Maximum cross-section: 9.5in × 9.7in (240 × 246mm)
Muzzle velocity: 3450ft/sec (1050m/sec)
Rate of fire: 1650–1850rds/min
Recoil load (standard muzzle): 22kN

SQUADRON SERVICE

Orders for RAF Harrier IIs currently total 96 aircraft, a first batch comprising two development and sixty production machines being supplemented by another 34 in an April 1988 contract. The first 41 aircraft have been delivered as 'straight' GR Mk 5s and Nos 42 to 62 as Mk 5As, fitted for (but not yet with) night attack equipment; the 63rd and subsequent aircraft are being rolled out as definitive GR Mk 7s, complete with FLIR installation, NGC cockpit and the rest. In the years ahead, all the GR.5s and 5As will be flown back to Dunsfold for modification into full GR.7 condition and the original mark will cease to equip front-line squadrons.

The first production aircraft was delivered to the RAF on 1 July 1987 and was taken on charge by the GR.5 Conversion Team (GR5CT), a specially formed unit within No 233 Operational Conversion Unit (OCU) at RAF Wittering. All eight GR5CT aircraft were on duty within eighteen months. Full conversion of the OCU proceeded alongside that of the first front-line unit, No 1(F) Squadron (co-located at RAF Wittering), whose GR.3s were all withdrawn by the spring of 1989. The next unit to

re-form with the Harrier II was No 3 Squadron, based at RAF Gutersloh in West Germany, and once conversion was complete the GR5CT was disbanded, its personnel re-absorbed into the OCU. The third (and presumably last) unit to convert will doubtless be the other GR.3 operator, No 4 Squadron at RAF Gutersloh, and it may be assumed that this will be the first to be equipped with the GR.7, later in 1990 or 1991.

Unlike their disruptive-camouflaged predecessors, Harrier IIs in the RAF are finished in a rather plain scheme of NATO Green IRR on the upper surfaces and Medium Green ('Chive') on the lower surfaces, both colours being matt polyurethane. The two development aircraft, ZD318 and 319, for some time wore a semi-matt polyurethane Dark Sea Grey and Medium Sea Grey paint finish, with glossy black nose undercarriage and forward access doors, presumably as a 'false canopy' device. The green scheme was adopted as standard following trials with GR.3s in West Germany in 1984 – which took place as the GR.5 paintwork drawings were being finalised – and night attack GR.7s are expected to be similarly finished.

Below: DB1 and DB2 (ZD318 and 319) were originally finished in a paint scheme comprising Dark Sea Grey (BS381C-638) and Medium Sea Grey (BS381C-637) – which might have become the standard RAF Harrier II colours had not the 1984 'Match Coat' trials in West Germany shown the alternative green scheme to be preferable. Note the glossy black panelling beneath the nose, doubtless a 'false canopy' to confuse would-be attackers had this become operational.

Below: A GR Mk 5 from No 233 OCU in the standard green scheme (see next spread). The fin code is white. The unit's wild cat markings are illustrated in colour on page 20.

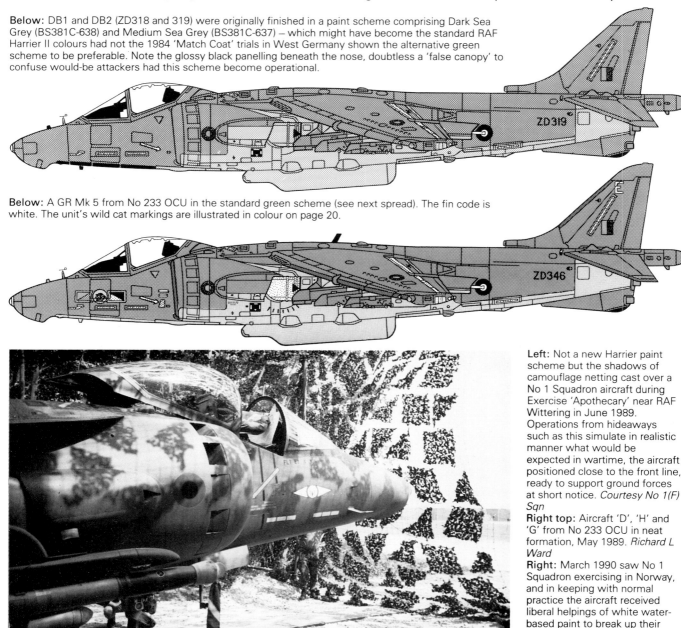

Left: Not a new Harrier paint scheme but the shadows of camouflage netting cast over a No 1 Squadron aircraft during Exercise 'Apothecary' near RAF Wittering in June 1989. Operations from hideaways such as this simulate in realistic manner what would be expected in wartime, the aircraft positioned close to the front line, ready to support ground forces at short notice. *Courtesy No 1(F) Sqn*

Right top: Aircraft 'D', 'H' and 'G' from No 233 OCU in neat formation, May 1989. *Richard L Ward*

Right: March 1990 saw No 1 Squadron exercising in Norway, and in keeping with normal practice the aircraft received liberal helpings of white water-based paint to break up their outlines against the wintry surroundings. *Phil Boyden/BAe*

BRITISH AEROSPACE HARRIER GR Mk 5, No 1(F) SQUADRON, RAF WITTERING, NOVEMBER 1988

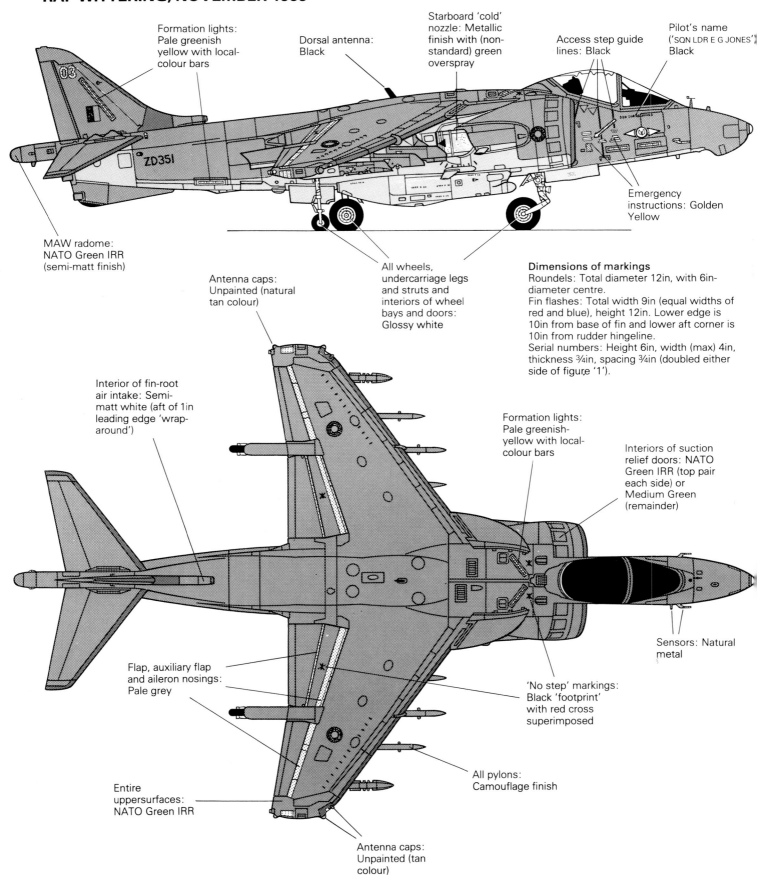

Formation lights: Pale greenish yellow with local-colour bars

Dorsal antenna: Black

Starboard 'cold' nozzle: Metallic finish with (non-standard) green overspray

Access step guide lines: Black

Pilot's name ('SQN LDR E G JONES') Black

Emergency instructions: Golden Yellow

MAW radome: NATO Green IRR (semi-matt finish)

Antenna caps: Unpainted (natural tan colour)

All wheels, undercarriage legs and struts and interiors of wheel bays and doors: Glossy white

Dimensions of markings
Roundels: Total diameter 12in, with 6in-diameter centre.
Fin flashes: Total width 9in (equal widths of red and blue), height 12in. Lower edge is 10in from base of fin and lower aft corner is 10in from rudder hingeline.
Serial numbers: Height 6in, width (max) 4in, thickness ¾in, spacing ¾in (doubled either side of figure '1').

Interior of fin-root air intake: Semi-matt white (aft of 1in leading edge 'wrap-around')

Formation lights: Pale greenish-yellow with local-colour bars

Interiors of suction relief doors: NATO Green IRR (top pair each side) or Medium Green (remainder)

Flap, auxiliary flap and aileron nosings: Pale grey

'No step' markings: Black 'footprint' with red cross superimposed

Sensors: Natural metal

All pylons: Camouflage finish

Entire uppersurfaces: NATO Green IRR

Antenna caps: Unpainted (tan colour)

British Standard Colour (BSC) references
Post Office Red: BS381C-538
Roundel Blue: BS381C-110
Golden Yellow: BS381C-356
Note: All colours, including principal camouflage paintwork, are matt polyurethane finish, except where noted in the labelling.

For further information about Harrier GR.5 colours and markings, reference to Modeldecal set 100 is recommended

1:72 scale

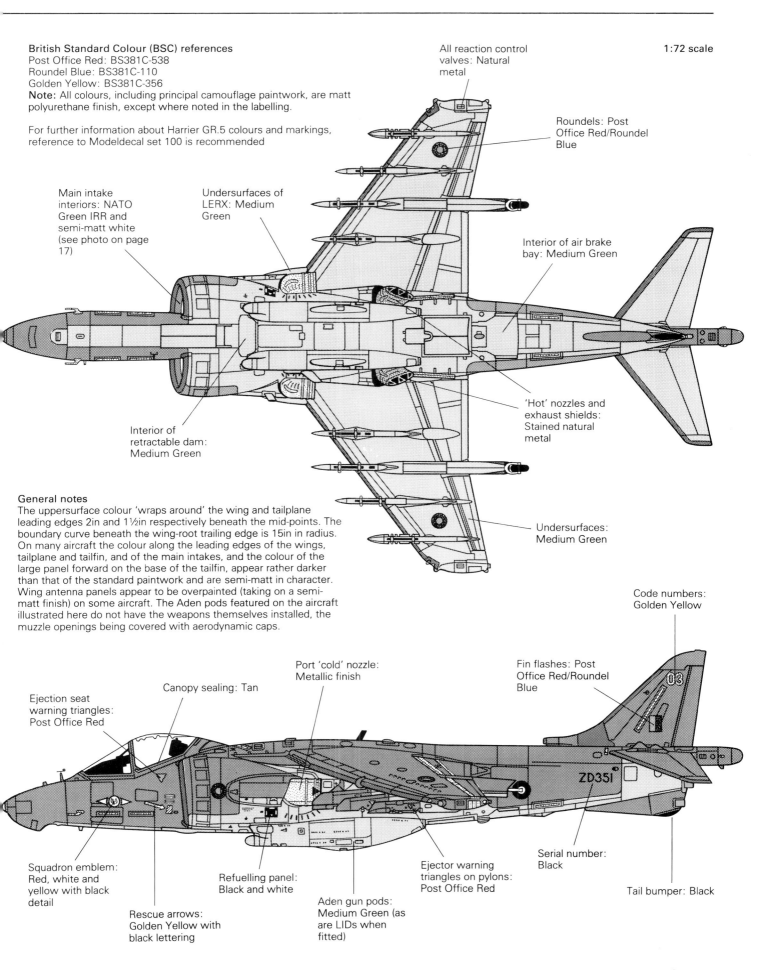

All reaction control valves: Natural metal

Roundels: Post Office Red/Roundel Blue

Main intake interiors: NATO Green IRR and semi-matt white (see photo on page 17)

Undersurfaces of LERX: Medium Green

Interior of air brake bay: Medium Green

Interior of retractable dam: Medium Green

'Hot' nozzles and exhaust shields: Stained natural metal

Undersurfaces: Medium Green

General notes
The uppersurface colour 'wraps around' the wing and tailplane leading edges 2in and 1½in respectively beneath the mid-points. The boundary curve beneath the wing-root trailing edge is 15in in radius. On many aircraft the colour along the leading edges of the wings, tailplane and tailfin, and of the main intakes, and the colour of the large panel forward on the base of the tailfin, appear rather darker than that of the standard paintwork and are semi-matt in character. Wing antenna panels appear to be overpainted (taking on a semi-matt finish) on some aircraft. The Aden pods featured on the aircraft illustrated here do not have the weapons themselves installed, the muzzle openings being covered with aerodynamic caps.

Code numbers: Golden Yellow

Port 'cold' nozzle: Metallic finish

Canopy sealing: Tan

Fin flashes: Post Office Red/Roundel Blue

Ejection seat warning triangles: Post Office Red

Squadron emblem: Red, white and yellow with black detail

Refuelling panel: Black and white

Rescue arrows: Golden Yellow with black lettering

Aden gun pods: Medium Green (as are LIDs when fitted)

Ejector warning triangles on pylons: Post Office Red

Serial number: Black

Tail bumper: Black

Below: The second front-line squadron to equip with the GR.5 was No 3, assigned to RAF Germany. The unit's famous cockatrice emblem with green and yellow flanking bars has been positioned on the front nozzle fairing; its GR.3s featured nose-mounted markings. The fin tip is also green and yellow, and the tail code letters are black.

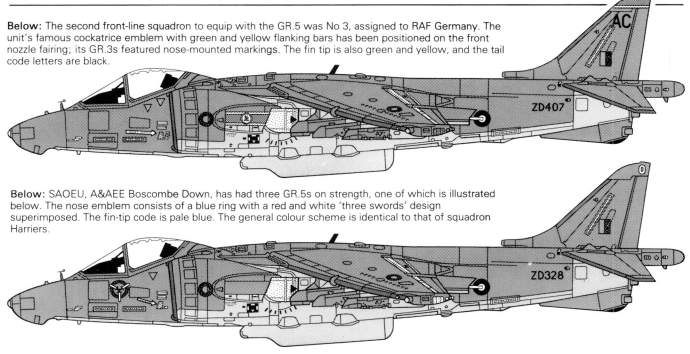

Below: SAOEU, A&AEE Boscombe Down, has had three GR.5s on strength, one of which is illustrated below. The nose emblem consists of a blue ring with a red and white 'three swords' design superimposed. The fin-tip code is pale blue. The general colour scheme is identical to that of squadron Harriers.

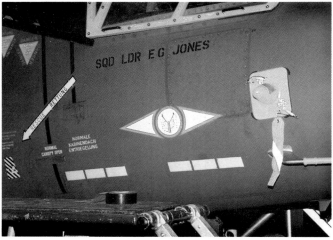

Above: A close-up view of ZD351/'03' (see pages 38–39) showing the emblem of No 1 Squadron, a red numeral '1' with yellow, white and black wing detail, with a red and white flanking design. The pilot's name is stencilled in black.

Above right: Detail showing the No 3 Squadron emblem, the cockatrice being pale blue and white with red comb and black detail, posed on a highlighted monolith (recalling the unit's early associations with Stonehenge on Salisbury Plain). Note the bolt-on semi-retractable refuelling probe. *Courtesy Alan Carlaw*

Below left: Individual aircraft of the OCU are readily identified by their fin code – a white letter in the range A–H.

Below centre: No 1 Squadron GR.5s originally sported a yellow numeral as a tail code, as here, but changed to a red numeral and then to a red numeral with a yellow outline by the time the unit became operational.

Below right: No 3 Squadron utilises paired letters in the 'AA', 'AB' etc range, painted black. It rather looks as though this particular aircraft – the Squadron's first GR.5 – was transferred from No 1 Squadron: an overpainted '04' code is discernible behind the letters. *Courtesy Alan Carlaw*

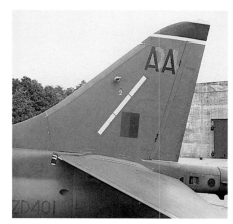